# St Paul's
# Olive Tree Metaphor

Unless otherwise stated, Bible quotations are from the New International Version, copyright 1973, 1978, International Bible Society. Published by Hodder &Stoughton. Used by permission.

Some footnoted variations from the N.I.V. text are included in quotations, using parentheses.

All photos used are in the public domain unless stated otherwise.

For Ruth.

This is what the Lord says. He who appoints the sun to shine by day, who decrees the moon and the stars to shine by night, who stirs up the sea so that its waves roar – the Lord Almighty is his name:

*"Only if these decrees vanish from my sight,"* declares the Lord, *"will the descendants of Israel ever cease to be a nation before me."*

This is what the Lord says.

*"Only if the heavens above can be measured*

*and the foundations of the earth below be searched out will I reject all the descendants of Israel because of all they have done,"*

declares the Lord.

(Jer. 31:35-37).

# Table of Contents

# Chapter 1: Introduction

# Chapter 1
# Introduction

This important section of the Epistle to the Romans, chapters nine, ten and eleven, is not an insignificant parenthesis in the main teaching of Romans, but is of major theological significance.

In the Hebrew Scriptures, (see Hos.14:6 and Jer.11:16), Israel is described as an olive tree. In these chapters of Romans, described by former Archbishop of Sydney, Donald Robinson, in his book "*Faith's Framework*" (p.110) as "*Paul's most important treatment of the dispensation of God in relation to the salvation of man-kind*" Paul utilises this same symbol: the olive tree. He provides a brief history of the people of Israel by means of the following simple pictorial description: Initially the Creator planted an Olive Tree. This Tree, which pictures the Chosen People of God, is not a wild olive tree, but a garden variety, cultivated for its oil and fruit. As in Jesus' parable of the fig tree, which failed to bring forth good fruit (Luk. 13:6-7), the Almighty, the Gardener, needed to take drastic action, in this case, to do some pruning. He cut off many branches of this Olive Tree; yet left some behind. He then grafted into the spaces so created, branches from a Wild Olive Tree, and the graft 'took'. The selection criterion was faith. If they possessed faith, both wild and cultivated branches were selected to be part of the Tree. The Gardener warned the engrafted branches not to be proud or arrogant towards the rejected branches, as they themselves could also be broken off, discarded from the Olive Tree.

The olive tree metaphor was developed by the Apostle Paul to convey his understanding of three relationships i.e., that between the Jewish and gentile followers of Jesus; that between those same Gentiles and Biblical Judaism; and that between the Jewish People and the God of Israel.

St Paul taught the duality of these two people-groups, Jews and Gentiles. That means that he did not advocate that Jewish believers should be submerged in a gentile matrix, assimilated into an undifferentiated gentilised Church, as was usually the case when Jews accepted Jesus as saviour.

At first glance, the following verse appears to contradict this key Pauline teaching from the Book of Romans, the key teaching conveyed by the Olive Tree metaphor:

*"There is neither Jew nor Greek, slave nor free, male nor female, for you are all one in Christ (Messiah) Jesus."* (Gal.3:28).

In reality, however, this verse actually illustrates Paul's belief; as follows.... When male and female become believers they do not change bodily shape or function. They continue to be easily identified as different, and continue to have differences in function; yet they are accorded the same spiritual standing before the Almighty.

Similarly St Paul would have been able to recognise a Christian slave from a freeman, by outward appearance and functional difference. Earthly status remained anything but identical, yet both were accorded the same spiritual standing before God. These same principles are applicable to Jewish and Greek (gentile) believers in Jesus. They had identical spiritual status, but were functionally different, just as male and female retain their differences, although their beliefs are the same.

St Paul frequently called Jews or Jewish believers 'the circumcision' and their gentile counterparts 'the uncircumcision'. This was a major difference between the two groups. Jewish believers, especially in Jerusalem, continued to observe Torah - the Covenant of Circumcision and the whole Law of Moses. Gentile believers, however, were not required to keep the whole Law of Mosees. Although there was some early controversy about whether gentiles must first convert to Judaism before becoming followers of Yeshua, who is called Jesus in English, the controversy was settled c.49 A.D. The decision, that this was unnecessary, was made by the apostles and leaders (or bishops), meeting as the First Council of Jerusalem. Minimal regulations and observances were imposed on gentile believers, by that Council; (see Acts.15:19-21).

St Paul indicates, in Galatians 3:28, that Jews and Gentiles were intended to be functionally different. The Jewish people have their own destiny and vocation within the `people of God'. Both peoples, however, have the same spiritual status before the Lord; irrespective of earthly status. Salvation through the Messiah is applicable to all, both Jew and Greek, as Isaiah stated:

> *"We all, like sheep, have gone astray, each of us has turned to his own way; and the Lord has lain on him the iniquity of us all."*
> *(Is.53:6)*

While `Jew' and `Greek' have a spiritual unity, they, like `male' and `female', have a functional disparity.

Turning again to Paul's letter to the Church at Rome, we find three major chapters devoted to the exposition of the Olive Tree metaphor. In Chapters 9 and 10 Paul speaks of his own love and anguish concerning his own people, the Jews. He speaks of election, of God's selection of both the Church and of Abraham's natural children - through Isaac and Jacob. He speaks of those whom God has chosen and prepared for His glory - from among the Jews and from among the Gentiles.

This is in fulfilment of the words of the Hebrew prophets who affirm that the same Lord blesses them equally, if they seek Him, as, for example in Jer.12:14-17, and as follows:

> *"Let no foreigner who has joined himself to the Lord say, `The Lord will surely exclude me from his people.'"* (Is.56:3)

Romans Chapter 11 is the culmination of Paul's teaching about the relationship between Jew and Gentile. It concludes with the truth that "all Israel will be saved". Expounding this truth moves Paul to such depths that he breaks out in the paeon of praise with which he concludes this segment:

> *"Oh, the depth of the riches of the wisdom and knowledge of God! How unsearchable his judgements; and his paths beyond tracing out!"* (Rom.11:33).

In speaking about the future salvation of Israel, Paul, in Romans chapter 11, verses 26-27, alludes to the following declarations from the prophet Isaiah:

> *"By this, then, will Jacob's guilt be atoned for, and this will be the full fruitage of the removal of his sin."* (Is.27:9a)

> *"'The Redeemer will come to Zion, to those in Jacob who repent of their sins,' declares the Lord. 'As for me, this is my covenant within them,' says the Lord. 'My Spirit who is on you, and my words that I have put in your mouth will not depart from your mouth, or from the mouths of your children, or the mouths of their descendants from this time on and forever,' says the Lord."* (Is.59:20-21)

By quoting from Isaiah, Paul is announcing that his theology on the issue of Israel is firmly based in the Old Testament and is firmly based in the prophetic message given to the Jewish people. He also affirms a belief in the covenants given to the Jewish people in times of old, including the covenant of their eternal relationship with God, and their redemption. Paul affirms that the Redeemer will indeed come to the people of Zion. He will come to those in Jacob (who was later called ' Israel', the father of the twelve tribes of Israel), who seek God, repenting of their sins.

Paul specifically stated that he was writing this, and explaining the mystery of Israel, because he did not wish his readers to be ignorant nor conceited (11:25). These are the reasons why we, also, should study this mystery.

**Plate 1. Olive tree outside Temple Mount.**

Photo: D. Campbell, 1988.

# Chapter 2
# Did God Reject Israel?

There is a common belief that God has rejected the Jewish people and that all the promises made to them in the Old Testament have now been transferred to the church, which is sometimes called 'Spiritual Israel' or the 'New Israel'. This position is widely accepted in many denominations. These are the modern anti-Semites in Christian garb, whose beliefs, unfortunately, have infiltrated Churches across the globe. A single quotation may serve to illustrate their attitude to God's Ancient Covenant People:

> *"God's people must not seek to reform Israel with its new religion of Judaism but abandon her to her fate."* (David Chiltern, "Days of Vengeance")

The views held by such exponents of replacement theology are grounded in neither History nor the Bible; and a plain and literal reading of the Bible undermines their case. They interpret 'the Land of Israel' to mean 'Christ' or 'the Spiritual Inheritance of the Church', thereby contravening the principle of Biblical interpretation that, if a literal interpretation fits and is meaningful, it is the correct interpretation. By spiritualising certain selected passages they ignore the fact that symbolic and metaphorical passages are in a separate and clearly identifiable category as allegorical prose. Clear principles of Biblical exegesis have to be abandoned in order to justify the 'replacement theology' position.

In failing to understand the place of Israel in the Lord's cosmology they are unable to work in harmony with His purposes. In their failure to understand that the Church is not a completely new body, but one which grew out of Israel, the Jewish scriptures, and Jewish moral law, they fail to understand both the Bible and historical truth. In coining the term 'the Judaeo-Christian ethic' the secular world demonstrates that it understands the historic basis of Christianity better than the Church, refusing to differentiate between the two because both are based on the Ten Commandments and Jewish morality, under the same God.

Those who claim that God's special purposes, His covenants, and His love for the Jewish people as His Own People ceased when Jesus came and 'fulfilled all things', 'instituted a new order' and 'appointed the Church to replace Israel' cannot claim to believe the Bible. They cannot claim that they accept New Testament doctrine and they cannot claim that they believe the Book of Romans. They cannot claim to follow the example and teaching of St. Paul in this epistle, because he wrote:

*"I ask then, Did God reject His people? By no means! ... God did not reject his people".* (Rom.11:1-2a)

If God HAD rejected His Ancient People and if the Church, a largely gentile church, was intended to replace the Jewish people, the Apostle Paul would have made that fact explicit in the Epistle to the Romans, a work in which he expounds the deepest principles of the Gospel. While speaking about Israel, using the metaphor of the Olive Tree, Paul would certainly have seized the opportunity to explain, if indeed he had believed it, that this Tree, which represents Israel, had been cut down and thrown away. The truth is that his teaching on the Olive Tree is quite the opposite.

By the date of the writing of this epistle, around 57 or 58 A.D., the Church had spread throughout most of the Roman world. Its offices and functions were established, its apostles acknowledged, its bishops appointed and its doctrines clarified, systematised and taught. 'Christian' attitudes to the Jewish people would have crystallised under the leadership of Jesus' original apostles, all of whom were Jews.

The Epistle to the Romans, and that to the Hebrews, which was probably written around 80 A.D. (certainly before 95 A.D.) provides strong Biblical evidence in favour of an on-going Divine purpose for the Jewish people, and against those forms of 'replacement theo-logy' which deny this purpose. Every Christian must confront the challenge of these long ignored New Testament scriptures openly and honestly. Romans must be encountered without prejudice.

The Bible affirms that while our universe remains, complete and ultimate rejection of Israel is impossible:

> *"This is what the Lord says: 'Only if the heavens above can be measured and the foundations of the earth below be searched out will I reject all the descendants of Israel because of all they have done', declares the Lord." (Jer.31:37) "'Only if these decrees (i.e., the physical laws of the universe) vanish from my sight,' declares the Lord 'will the descendants of Israel ever cease to be a nation before me'"* (v.36)

The Bible also teaches that, despite years, or indeed centuries, of discipline and punishment, there would come a time when God would again look on Zion with warmth and compassion:

> *"You will arise and have compassion on Zion, for it is time to show favour to her; the appointed time has come."* (Ps.102:13)

Christians may disagree as to the timing of this day of mercy for Israel but they cannot deny that such a time exists, because the Epistle to the Romans makes unequivocal statements about God's continuing concern for Israel's physical and spiritual welfare. The Apostle Paul begins the eleventh chapter by asking:

*"Did God reject his people?"* (Rom.11:1)

He immediately goes on to provide the answer to his own question:

*"By no means! .... God did not reject his people."* (Rom.11:1-2a)

This chapter addresses the very question of the ultimate fate of the Jewish people, their ultimate acceptance, or rejection. Paul asks a most significant second question:

*"Again I ask, Did they stumble so as to fall beyond recovery?"* (Rom.11:11)

This second question, so similar to Paul's first, serves to emphasise and reinforce the point. We are left in no doubt as to Paul's meaning. Obviously his answer to the second question is similar to his previous answer:

*"Not at all!"* (Rom.11:11)

They did not fall beyond recovery! As will be shown, the Apostle Paul concurs with what the Old Testament, the Tenach, has always taught, that the Lord will never reject His ancient chosen people, nor ever forsake His inheritance, Israel.

# Chapter 3
# The First Metaphor

In the Epistle to the Romans we find two distinct metaphors which use `tree' images. In order to understand the full weight of Paul's teaching about the Jewish people these metaphors must not be confused. One metaphor is that of the Olive Tree which St.Paul likens to Israel. In chapter eleven he describes both natural olive branches, which are the Jewish people, and wild olive branches, which clearly represent the Gentiles. He speaks about the grafting process. This process is well understood in agricultural societies, but Paul reverses the imagery.

**Plate 2: Olive branch by Glenda Valais.**

The usual grafting of olive trees is similar to that of rose bushes, in that the more vigorous wild variety is always used to provide a root system, whereas the more delicate, propagated variety is grafted onto that root to provide for a quality fruit, or quality flowers, nourished by hardy root stock. In reversing the imagery, Paul describes the grafting into a cultivated root of wild branches, which represent the Gentiles. He also compares the greater ease with which the cultivated branches may be regrafted into their own root system, when compared with the difficulty of grafting a foreign wild branch into the Olive Tree. The meaning of this comparison is that it is generally easier for Jewish people to be part of "the people of God" than for formerly heathen people from among the gentiles to be part of that Holy People.

Despite the unusual reversal of the grafting metaphor, Paul's meaning is quite clear. Paul's metaphor vividly portrays how life flows from the parent plant, the root system, into the branches - both foreign and natural. Sap flows out through the grafted branches in just the same measure and quality as through any remaining natural branches. By this Paul means that the root system of Israel supports and nourishes the gentile believer in the God of Israel.

*"If some of the branches have been broken off, and you, though a wild olive shoot, have been grafted in among the others and now share in the nourishing sap from the olive root, do not boast over those branches. If you do, consider this; You do not support the root, but the root supports you."* (Rom.11:17-18)

Some readers confuse 'the Olive Tree metaphor' with the metaphor of 'the vine and the branches', and thereby misinterpret Paul's meaning in Romans. In Romans 11 Paul is not teaching that Jesus is 'the root', but that the Jewish race is the root of the Olive Tree. The Olive Tree metaphor, itself, come from the Old Testament, (Hos.14:6; Jer.11:16).

Can we be sure that the 'root' in this metaphor is the Jewish people? Yes, the meaning is quite clear, that initially the cultivated branches and the root are one and the same tree. The root and the remaining branches continue to be part of that original tree. Later the `nourishing sap', from that very same root, supports both types of branches.

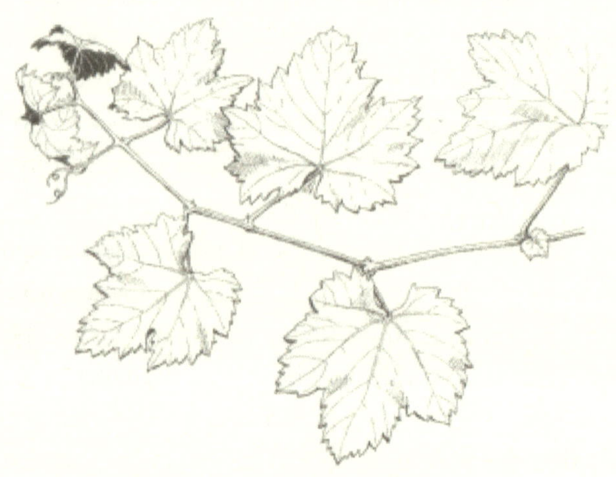

**Plate 3: Grape-vine branch by Glenda Valais.**

Paul develops the question of the fate of some of the natural branches. Some, but not all of the Jewish race, were cut off. Early in Chapter 11 Paul affirms that the Jewish people are not rejected and have NOT fallen beyond recovery; while later in the chapter he explains that they are still loved by God, Who has not changed His mind about His choice of them.

> *"From the point of view of God's choice - of election, of divine selection - they are still the beloved (dear to Him) for the sake of their forefathers (the Patriarchs). For God's gifts and His call are irrevocable - He never withdraws them when once they are given, and he does not change His mind about those to whom He gives His grace or to whom He sends His call."* (Rom.11:28b-29.Amp.)

God cannot reject the Jewish people because He cannot deny His own character as a keeper of covenants, a keeper of all of His good promises.

*"...he is the faithful God, keeping his covenant of love to a thousand generations" (Deut.7:9)*

The Lord cannot deny Himself, nor does He wish too. No matter what they do, for the sake of the faithful saints of the Old Testament and the Patriarchs, He will keep faith with His First and Ancient Covenant People. It is most important for gentile believers to understand the Divine perspective, and to share His attitudes.

In so far as some original branches were cut off, in order to allow for the grafting in of wild branches, Paul warns gentile readers not to have an arrogant attitude to the fate of those Jewish people disconnected from their own Olive Tree, lest a similar fate befall the proud. How much easier is it for this fate to befall Gentiles, who were originally outside of the Commonwealth of Israel!

Here Paul also teaches that gratitude and humility should be given to the Jewish people, an admonition that is often simply neglected or deliberately rejected. WE should remember that it is from them, the Bible tells us, that we have received these things:

*"Theirs is the adoption as sons, theirs the divine glory, the covenants, the receiving of the law, the temple worship and the promises. Theirs are the patriarchs, and from them is traced the human ancestry of Christ..." (Rom.9:4-5a)*

It was the Rabbi Paul, more correctly Sh'aul - who asked: If the cutting off of some of the natural branches resulted in the birth of the Church:

*"What will their acceptance be but life from the dead?"*
(Rom.11:15)

He did not say "what might it be" as though there is any possibility that they might not be accepted. Paul believed that Israel WILL have a day of spiritual fullness in the future, a time of great spiritual riches. He asked:

*"How much greater riches will their fullness bring?"*
(Rom.11:12b)

There is no sense of `maybe' or `perhaps' in Paul's belief that their fullness, their ingathering, their faith, WILL bring greater riches to the world.

In this epistle the apostle makes a powerful, inescapable and definitive statement about God's future plans and purposes for the Jewish people:

*"And so all Israel will be saved."* (Rom.11:26)

This promise is a confirmation of the Old Testament covenants with Israel.

When these words were written, about 58 A.D. Jesus had been crucified and the Church had already been well established, and yet Paul was writing of Israel, not in the past tense but in a future tense. He was speaking of a FUTURE for Israel, which at that time had not yet come to pass. In other words Paul was looking forward to a future time when all Israel will be saved. Paul's conviction, his prophetic vision for Israel, belies the teaching that God has finished with the Jewish people. On the contrary it affirms a beautiful ultimate purpose in God's plan, which we know will accord with what they have been promised in their own Scriptures, the Tenach.

**Plate 4. Olive Trees, Gethsemane.**
**Photo: Ian Finnin, 2018.**

# Chapter 4
# What of Spiritual Israel ?

The term `Spiritual Israel' is not a Biblical term and there is no developed scriptural teaching on `Spiritual Israel'. It is a non-biblical term used of the Church. The Church certainly is a spiritual entity, but it is NOT, of itself, Israel. The term `Spiritual Israel' encapsulates a major tenant of the `replacement theology' position. It suggests that there are two Israels; one physical, the other spiritual - one described in the Old Testament and one in the New.

Having become convinced of the existence of these two Israels it is an easy step to believe that God has transferred to the second of these all of His promises and commitments to the first. The truth however is that these very promises and commitments contain within them the assurance that they are eternal and irrevocable and that they belong to those very people to whom they were first made. This concept of their irrevocability is confirmed in the New Testament. They are confirmed by Paul, the `Apostle to the Gentiles' himself:

> *"They (the Jewish race) are still the beloved (dear to Him) for the sake of their fore-fathers. For God's gifts and His call are irrevocable - He never withdraws them when once they are given, and He does not change His mind about those to whom He gives His grace or to whom He sends His call."* (Rom.11:28b-29.Amp.)

Many times throughout the Old Testament the terms `eternal', `everlasting' and `for ever' are used when speaking about God's promises to Abraham, Isaac, Jacob, David and to the people of Israel in general.

The teachings of 'replacement theology' deny the truth of all these Scriptures.

The Apostle Paul had a very literal view of Israel. For him Israel was historic Israel. For example, he was not speaking about the Church, a 'spiritual Israel', when he proudly spoke of his own racial identity:

> *"I am an Israelite myself, a descendant of Abraham from the tribe of Benjamin."* (Rom.11:1)

Could he possibly have been speaking of a 'New Israel', the Church, when he wrote:

> *"Brothers, my heart's desire and prayer to God for the Israelites is that they may be saved."* (Rom.10:1)

Of course not! It would be nonsense for Paul's greatest desire to be the salvation of the Church which he knew.

Why not? Because the Epistle to the Romans was written only about twenty five years after Jesus' resurrection and most of the members of the Church in the city of Rome had previously been pagan and all of its members, like those of the wider Church, would have been recently converted first generation believers. It is impossible that Paul meant that he was longing for the salvation of this particular Church, or even the wider Church. Surely Paul would not have regarded their salvation as being in doubt!

If, by any chance, Paul did mean 'the Church' when he said 'Israel', then certain of these verses become preposterous defamations of that Church. Could Paul possibly have meant:-

> *"But not all of the (spiritual) Israelites (i.e., the Church) accepted the good news"* (as Romans 10:16 could be so interpreted)??

He could not have been referring to the Church because they HAD all accepted the good news. How else could they have qualified, at that early date, as belonging to the Church? There simply were no nominal or second generation members.

Consider also how Romans 10:21 could be interpreted by `replacement' theologians:-

> "`*But concerning (spiritual) Israel (the Church)' he says `All day long I have held out my hands to a disobedient and obstinate people*'".

Could it possibly be that the early Church was a disobedient and obstinate people who rejected God ??

If Paul intended the word `Israel' to mean `the Church' then neither of these two statements from Romans Chapter 10 makes any sense in a first century context where recently baptised first generation converts received their instruction in the faith directly from Paul and the other Apostles and in the power of the Holy Spirit faced threats of immanent persecution; even joyfully accepting death for the Lord's sake.

Paul would not have used the label `Israel' to mean the Jewish people in some sections of this epistle and to mean the Church in others, and then vice versa, without first indicating that he was changing the use of the term. Paul was a logical, intelligent, and inspired thinker, with a thorough theological education under one of Judaism's greatest rabbis, Gamaliel I. As we would expect, his argument is well developed, logical and conclusive.

The whole of this section of Romans combines to form a cohesive teaching, and, if each and every use of the word `Israel' is taken to mean the Jewish people, the historical Israel, it makes perfect sense. The logical and inescapable conclusion is that the Apostle Paul did not use the term `Israel' to mean the Church, or `Spiritual Israel', in any part of this epistle. He was speaking of the Jewish people, the Israelites, in the post-resurrection, post-Pentecost period: moreover Paul's use of terminology remains consistent throughout the Epistle.

We have to assume that Paul meant Israel when he wrote 'Israel', otherwise this Epistle, rather than being a classic exposition of Christian doctrine, becomes indecipherable confusion - which it certainly is not. Theologians throughout the centuries have had the greatest admiration for Romans, and for its teaching. It underpinned much Protestant theology, and was a foundation upon which the theological understanding of the major protestant thinkers was built. John Calvin called it "*the door to the rarest treasures of scripture*" and John Knox called it "*the most important theological book ever written*".

It was through reading the Epistle to the Romans that Martin Luther came to an understanding of 'justification by faith', an understanding from which the Protestant Reformation grew. This epistle, therefore, had a special and personal significance to Luther, who called it: "the chief book of the New Testament and the purest Gospel."

For the believer of today, also, the Book of Romans should be foundational. Its doctrine in regard to the Jewish people is central and irrefutable. Its entire message must be examined both thoroughly and honestly.

# Chapter 5
# Lost In Time

Paul's systematic teaching in Romans, of the separate identity of the two Olive Trees, the primacy of the Cultivated Olive and the dependence upon it of the Wild Olive branches, is of such authority and stature that major questions beg to be answered.

Why, how and when was this teaching lost? Why is it being either ignored or refuted in mainstream Christianity throughout the world today ? Five forces appear to have combined together to bring about the effective loss of this Pauline doctrine. Some of these forces are historic, some theological:

1) The dispersion of the original Jerusalem Church after the destruction of Jerusalem in 70 A.D.

2) The influence of the Early Church Fathers

3) The Influence of the 4$^{th}$ Century Bishops and Leaders

4) The Influence of the Early Christian Emperors

5) The influence of Medieval superstition and ignorance

6) The influence of the Reformation and Catholic Counter-Reformation.

7) The influence of the Authorised Version of the Bible

8) The spirit of anti-Semitism in the world

**1) Destruction and Dispersion.**

In the forty years between the Day of Pentecost and the Roman capture of Jerusalem in 70 A.D. the Jerusalem church consisted of those disciples who had personally known Jesus, local residents of the three thousand who came to faith through the preaching of Peter on the Day of Pentecost, and those others who were daily being added to the original number. The Church was led by Peter, Jesus' brother James, and John, son of Zebedee. Some others of the original Apostles also remained in Jerusalem.

Various Scriptures indicate that these Apostles continued to observe the Law of Moses, the Torah, and to maintain their Jewish lifestyle, (see Acts 10:14 & 11:2 & 15:5).

Their authority in other churches was acknowledged. Even the Apostle Paul went up to Jerusalem to submit, first himself, and later his teachings and his mission, to their authority, (see Act.9:26-30 & 15:4). It was at Jerusalem that all the bishops met in Council, in about 49 A.D., under the presidency of James, to decide whether or not gentile believers must observe Jewish Law (see Act.15:6-21). Peter and James remained in Jerusalem, even during times of severe persecution. The doctrine which emanated from the apostolic seat in Jerusalem, and which would have been in harmony with the Epistle to the Romans, was firmly grounded in Jesus' life and teaching, and in the Hebrew Scriptures. James, called `The Just' and `The Righteous', lived as a Nazarite, admired even by Temple authorities for his life of purity and prayer, until his martyrdom at their hands (although there are two accounts of his death: that of Bishop Eeusebius and that of the Jewish historian, Josephus).

In 70 A.D., as Titus and the Tenth Roman Legion marched down from the North, members of the Church in Jerusalem fled across the Jordan River to the region of Pella. They escaped the carnage in the city by heeding Jesus' warnings which told them that when they see:

*"... Jerusalem surrounded by armies, you will know that its desolation is near. Then let those who are in Judea flee to the mountains, let those who are in the city get out"*. (Luk.21:20)

After Jerusalem was destroyed by the Legions, on the ninth day of the Jewish month of Av, Temple Mount was left with no stone upon another. It is said that the stones were pulled apart to obtain the gold which melted and ran into the cracks between them. Only the massive Temple platform, of which the Western Wall is a part, and Herod's triple towers near todays Jaffa Gate, remained standing when the Legionaries had taken all their plunder.

Believers were scattered among the nations, along with the Jewish survivors of the city's destruction - survivors of the fires, the pillage, the torture and the imprisonments. Later, in 135 A.D., after the Bar-Cochba revolt, all Jews were expelled from the area of Jerusalem: the Jewish Diaspora, their long years of dispersion, had begun.

Most of the Apostles had suffered martyrdom by 70 A.D.: James ('The Just') in 62, Paul in c.67 and Peter between 64 and 68 A.D. James was the first of a succession of fifteen bishops of Jerusalem, all of them ' of the Circumcision'. Eusebius, in his "History of the Church", tells us that:

> *"at that time (before 135 A.D.) their whole church consisted of Hebrew believers who had continued from apostolic times down to the later siege in which the Jews, after revolting a second time from the Romans, were overwhelmed in a full-scale war".*

From this time onwards the Church grew without the presence of the Apostles, in societies dominated by Gentiles. Members of those churches composed largely of Jewish believers were seen as part of the now disadvantaged and persecuted Jewish minority, as the earliest Church was seen as a sect of Judaism. In other congregations Jewish members were outnumbered by gentile members, whose culture overwhelmed the Hebrew ethos in which the original Church had been born and had, for a century, flourished. From this time onwards, a thorough grounding in the Hebrew Scriptures was generally absent, and Christianity began to have a distinctly gentile flavour and orientation.

## 2) The Influence of the Church Fathers.

Many of the Apostolic Fathers and Church Fathers of the second and third centuries A.D., who took the Church into the next generations, were of heathen (rather than Hebrew) birth, and many of them were learned in Greek philosophy. This facilitated the introduction of the faith to the many gentile nations of the Roman Empire, dominated as it was by Greek culture, thought and education. Unfortunately it also opened the way for heresies, such as Gnosticism, and for Hellenistic attitudes and theological perspective to permeate the Church. The canon of Scripture had not been established and counterfeit and spurious writings were circulating, in competition with the genuine writings of the Apostles.

Among the dubious writings circulating before the 3$^{rd}$ Century were apocryphal Acts of Peter, John, Andrew, Thomas and Paul; many counterfeit epistles; and gospels such as the Gospels of Bartholomew, Peter, Thomas, and Philip plus an Infancy Gospel called *The Book of James and/*or *the Protevangelium of James"*, with its fanciful legends about the Virgin Mary. All these were eventually rejected because of marked or minor heretical leanings, but it is no wonder that many strange ideas were held, even by those with respected authority in the Church.

Anti-Semitism increased with what is called 'the parting of the ways'. This began as soon as the Apostolic Age finished, that is about 100 A.D.

## A.  BARNABAS (between 70 and 200 A.D.)

Barnabas may have been a person's name or a pseudonym, used by someone impersonating the Apostle Barnabas. *The Epistle of Barnabas* was widely influential and demonstrates that the Church and Judaism were already far apart. This epistle criticised post-destruction Judaism (that is, rabbibic Judaism) using a collection of previously collated 'proof texts', which indicated that at least some Christians were deliberately separating themselves from Jews.

## B. MARCION (d.160A.D.)

Marcion was excommunicated in 144 A.D. but was highly successful in recruiting followers and his ideas were very influential. He taught that the Gods of the Hebrew and Christian Scriptures were not the same. He rejected the Old Testament, three of the Gospels and all books with a strongly Jewish flavour.

## C. JUSTIN MARTYR (c.100-165 A.D.)

Justin, one of the greatest apologists, was tolerant towards those Jewish believers who maintained their traditions. Unlike some, he did not exclude them from fellowship but he believed that Jews hated Christians. Justin laid foundations for Christian anti-Semitism in his *"Dialogue with Trypho the Jew"*, written to explain three main ideas, two of which demean the importance of Israel:

1. That the Old Covenant was transitory.
2. The Identity of the Logos with the God of the Old Testament.
3. That God intends the Gentiles to take the place of Israel.

## D. MELITO of SARDIS (d.190 A.D.)

Since the 1940's an important twentieth-century influence has been the discovery, and academic study of part of a previously lost work of Melito, Bishop of Sardis. This treatise on The Lord's Passion was not originally written for academic purposes but was devotional in intent and written in idiomatic language for the common people. Melito's prolific writings, his common touch, and the act that Sardis was an important episcopal see, ensured that his treaties would have been very influential in their day.

Melito rejected the Jews as *"Christ-slayers"*. He saw ancient Israel as the *"type"*, whereas the Church was the *"substance"*, the reality. From this era onwards, Christianity came to be called *"the New Covenant"*. Like other second century bishops in Asia Minor, Melito continued to celebrate Easter at the original time, to coincide with Passover, in the tradition of Philip the evangelist, John the Apostle and his protege - the saintly martyr, Polycarp, Bishop of Smyrna. Little is known of what Melito taught about the Sabbath as his treatise on Sunday has been lost.

## E. ORIGEN (185-254 A.D.)

The controversy about Origen, for example, despite his scholarship and wide influence, continued for three hundred years after his death. His teachings were finally condemned in 553 A.D., by the Fifth General Council, but not before he had undermined belief in the reign of the Messiah on Earth, which early writers such as Papias (d.130), Justin Martyr (d.165), Irenaeus (d.200) and Hippolytus of Rome (d.236) had taught.

Denial of the 'Millennium', the future earthly reign of Christ, did considerable damage to the doctrine of the importance of Israel and Jerusalem. This exacerbated the shift away from an interest in earthly Jerusalem. This shift was understandable as, by then, Jerusalem had been replaced by a Roman city, with a completely gentile population.

A shrine to the Roman god, Jupiter Capitolina, stood on Mt.Moriah, where once the Temple had stood. (Although in the 4th century the Christian Emperor Constantine I restored the Biblical name, Jerusalem.)

When Origen's four volume exposition of Christian doctrine, *De Principiis*, was translated into Latin by St. Jerome, a former supporter, Jerome came to believe that Origen was a heretic: but this work, the first great systematic exposition of Christianity, was available in Greek, and was even more influential once Jerome's highly regarded Latin translation had been completed. There was a protracted controversy about Origenism in the 4th century.

## F. ST CYPRIAN of CARTHAGE (d.258)

This very influential and highly regarded bishop was much influenced by fellow African, Tertullian (c.180-c.220) who became a heretic. In doctrine Carthage was closely associated with the bishop of

Rome, except for Bishop/Pope Stephen. Cyprian wrote not one but three books *adversus Judaeos* (against the Jews).

## 3) The 4ᵗʰ Century Bishops and Leaders

.The Church Fathers of the 4ᵗʰ Century form of group of teachers and leaders who were even more violently hostile to Jews, among them are St Jerome, St John Chrysostom, St Ambrose of Milan and St Augustine of Hippo.

### i) St Jerome (c.342-420)

Jerome was a prolific and influential writer and an acknowledge Bible scholar, but he was an abbot in Bethlehem and not a bishop. His greatest contribution was to translate the Greek and Hebrew Scriptures into Latin, a task in which he was assisted by a Jew. Yet he had a very low opinion of Jews and believed that there could never be expiation for them for erasing Christ. He taught that it was a Christian duty to always hate the Jews because God hated the Jews.

### ii) St John Chrysoston (c. 345-407)

Although John, called Chrysostom (Golden Mouth), became Patriarch of Constantinople and was the most able preacher of Eastern Christianity, he was far from circumspect in his writing, his preaching, or his relationships. He accused the Jews of the assassination of Christ, calling them *"most miserable and abandoned by God"*.

### iii) St Ambrose of Milan (c.339-397)

Ambrose, a Doctor of the Church, was a great theologian who led a mob that destroyed a synagogue.

### iv) St Augustine of Hippo

Augustiune, Bishop of Hippo in North Africa, said that the Jews began as sons of God but became sons of Satan.

## 4) Early Christian Emperors

Christianity became an accepted religion under the Emperor Constantine, who converted from paganism in 312 A.D. (although some historians continue to believe that Constantine's conversion was just a political convenience). Christianity was made the official State Religion by Emperor Theodosius I in 381, after which various types of compulsion were brought against the Jews. Once Christianity became the official religion of the Roman Empire anti-Semitism began to flourish, even in the Church. This made a careful assessment of St Paul's teaching most difficult, as purely political considerations dominated the church.

## Some Acts of Early Christian Emperors

Religious affairs became official business as Constantine I and subsequent Christian emperors became increasingly involved and Jews became more significant to Christian emperors's rule. Generally, the more Christianised a region became the more hostile the State was towards Jews and their institutions.

Christian Emperors began to dismantle rights that Jews had been accorded previously and to enhance the legal position of Christianity. In 321 A.D. Constantine I made Sunday a day of rest from work and then he made Christianity an official religion, in 325 A.D. Christianity triumphed under Emperor Theodosius II.

Theodosius II and Justinian codified Roman law for Christianity, disadvantaging Jews, notably if Jew's previous privileges impacted Christians, as in the case of slave-ownership.

From 527 to 565, the Emperor Justinian's laws protected apostate Jews, while tempting Jews with inducements, encouraging conversion to Christianity.

    i.  In 315 Constantine I forbad conversion to Judaism
    ii.  In 321 Chionstantine I made Sunday, not the Shabbath, a day of rest.
    iii.  In 339, Constantius forbad Jews to own Christian slaves or to marry Christian women.
    iv.  In 439, Theodosius II imposed civil and political disabilities on Jews, discouraging business relations with them.
    v.  In 440 Theodosius II forbad the building of new synagogues.
    vi.  In c.550 Justinian imposed legal disabilities on Jews.

## Laws of the Theodisian and Justiniatic Codes

(i) Jews and Christians may not intermarry (Theodosian Code 3.7.2; Justinian Code 1.9.2).

(ii) Christian conversion to Judaism was forbidden. (Theodosian Code 16.8.7; Justinian Code 1.7.1). Those who performed circumcisions were to be executed: the same punishment as for castration.

(iii) Jews must not own Christian slaves (Theodosian Code 16.9.1; Justinian Code 1.10.1) but the penalty was relatively light.

(iv) In 438 A.D. Jews who converted a Christian slave would be subject to both confiscation of property and the death penalty (Theodosian Code 48 and 54)

(v) Church buildings were recognised as sanctuaries for runaway Christian slaves (Theodosian Code 39; Justinian Code 61).

vi) In 584 the Talmud and rabbinic exegesis were prohibited.

vii) In 787, the Second Council of Nicaea excommunicated Christians who would not renounce Sabbath and other 'Judaising' observances.

Efforts were made to prevent Christians being converted to Judaism but conversion of Jews to Christianity were not unknown. Efforts to convert Jews and pagans to Christianity could include forced baptisms, which occurred *"in many communities throughout the empire, when local religious enthusiasm fanned by clergymen erupted into violence against non-Christians."*

As the Christian Byzantine Empire began to shrink in size and power Emperor Heraclius decreed forced baptism of Jews and polytheists in the 630s (although intermittently enforced). Leo III in 721-2, Basil in c.873-4 and by Romanos I (919-44) also imposed forced baptism. During much of the period under review Jews in the Christian East experienced intolerance, although there were two and a half centuries of undisturbed toleration just before the Crusades. The Crusades of the 12$^{th}$ and 13$^{th}$ centuries saw Western Europeans engage in widespread slaughter of Jews, Muslims ans even Eastern Christians.

## The Christian Struggle Agains Heresies

During the first four hundred years of Church history, the martyrdom of the Apostles and the demise of the Jerusalem Church. A wide variety of anti-Jewish teachings were developed and spread. These various factors combined with imperial patronage of the Church to prepare the way for later negative attitudes. All of the Apostles and the earliest believers were Jews but gentile members gradually began to predominate, which resulted in false teaching as Bishop Eusebius of Caesarea wrote, in about 310 A.D., in *The History of the Church*:

*"When the sacred band of the apostles had in various ways reached the end of their life, and the generations of those privileged to listen with their own ears to the Divine wisdom had passed on, then godless error began to take shape, through the deceit of false teachers, who, now that none of the apostles was left*

*threw of the mask and attempted to counter the preaching of the truth by teaching the knowledge falsely so called."*

## 5) Medieval Superstition and Ignorance.

Today, in westernised nations, it is impossible to comprehend the narrow mind-sets, the sheer ignorance, the physical restrictions and the spiritual gloom in which the vast mass of people were held when Europe was emerging from the Dark Ages. Even the most basic education and literacy was kept exclusively within church institutions. The common people were a prey to exploitation, corruption, lies, rumour and superstitions, and could be whipped into religious fanaticism and emotional extremes at the mere whim of unscrupulous or misguided religious and secular leaders.

It was in this climate, in Norwich, on Easter Saturday 1144, that the 'ritual murder accusation', that Jews crucified Christian children in mockery of Christ's passion, was created around the death of St. William of Norwich.

Persecutions across England seemed justified when the death of 'Little St. Hugh of Lincoln' was similarly interpreted. This anti-Semitic superstition, fanned by religious passions, and crusading zeal, quickly spread across southern England, resulting in the massacre of whole Jewish communities, and in rampant xenophobia. In 1190 a two day massacre of Jews in London and in many provincial cities broke out on the Coronation Day of Richard the Lion-heart. Shortly afterwards, arson in York's Jewish quarter left 150 Jews dead, their wealth stolen from the safekeeping of the Cathedral.

In 1275 England's Jews were forced to wear the 'badge of shame' which Pope Innocent had introduced. In England's case it was not a 'Star of David' but a yellow badge, shaped like the 'Two Tablets of Stone'. In 1278 six hundred Jewish heads of families were arrested, almost three hundred of them being hanged as criminals, their wealth seized by the crown.

Having been reduced to poverty, by royal taxes and employment restrictions, the Jews were expelled from England by the crusader king, Edward I, on the 9th day of Av, 1290; an expulsion which lasted for almost 400 years. It was not until 1885 that Jewish citizens of Britain were finally granted complete educational, economic and civil rights.

After a twelfth century Bishop of Norwich visited the Continent the ritual murder accusation spread to Europe as the 'blood libel'. This allegation, that Jews used the blood of Christian children at Passover, soon led to a massacre of the Jews of Blois, in France, and other terrible consequences. It became the pretext for Europe's pogroms and massacres and later was a 'justification' for Nazi atrocities. To this very day its shadow persists in unsophisticated and bigoted communities in Eastern and Western Europe, notably in Germany and Russia.


## 6) The Reformation and Counter-Reformation

Attitudes to Jewish people, which led to their expulsion from most of Western Europe between 1290 and 1492, had an effect, however indirect, on attitudes to a correctly pro-Jewish interpretation of the Bible. Despite rarely meeting a Jew the Protestant Reformers, especially Luther, were greatly concerned with Jews and Judaism. They criticised Jewish interpretations of Scripture because that undermined or challenged their own interpretations: a real threat because Scripture was the foundation of their teaching and of primary importance to their anti-Catholic stance.

The continuation of Medieval anti-Semitism influenced Christian attitudes to those Jewish believers who resisted absorption into the Church, the early 'Messianic Jews', and to those, such as the Spanish 'Marranos', who accepted forced conversion rather than death, but who tried to maintain aspects of their Jewish heritage.

Amongst Europe's Protestants the most infamous contribution was made by its founding father, Martin Luther (1483-1546), who initially was unprejudiced, and, in 1523, wrote *"Jesus Was Born a Jew"*. He hoped to convert the Jews, but in 1543, in bitter disappointment or because he was old and irritable, he wrote his virulent work *"From the Jews and Their Lies?"* He called Jews *"Christ-slayers"*, *"thirsty for money"*, *"live devils"*, *"a cursed and rejected race"* and an *"unbearable, devilish burden"*. Martin Luther advocated burning their synagogues and covering the remains with mud in order to *"honour God and Christianity"* and to break down and destroy their homes and then house them in stalls like gypsies. Further disabilities were recommended: removing their books; killing rabbis who taught, or prayed publicly; restricting their movement in public; forbidding usuary (charging interest, often Jews' only permitted source of income) and working them very hard (Hans Jansen, 'The Historical Roots of the Anti-Israel Position of Liberal Protestant Churches').

Luther repented of this attitude in his last days, but not before much damage had been done, notably in Germany, where, tragically, Luther's writings, mixed with nationalistic sentiment, later served as a convenient pretext in Hitler's hands. Hitler and Goebbels freely quoted Luther to explain (or excuse) their actions. Daphne Olsen's thesis clearly states, *"Luther laid the foundation for Hitler's holocaust"* (see bibliography below).

Luther's close associate, Philipp Melanchthon, thought that Jews and Judaism were anachronistic.

John Calvin (1509-1564) was ambiguous about Jews. He considered Judaism to be archaic (anachronistic) and taught that the Church (including Jewish-Christians) is *"the true Israel"*, which inherits God's promises. When Calvin arrived in Geneva the Jews had been expelled (in 1490/91), a ban which he did not reverse but, if a Jew needed to enter the city, a fee had to be paid. Calvin called Jews *"mad dogs"*, *"beasts"* and *"animals"* but regarded Old Testament Jews favourably and that God's covenant with them remains eternal. He used Old Testament theology to opine that only Jews who believed in Jesus Christ remained in the covenant, so that the Church was the faithful remnant and therefore the "True Israel". Calvin believed, however, in the ongoing possibility of Jews' salvation, even of all Jews' redemption.

Luther and Calvin promoted the perception of Jews as stubborn, blind and disobedient. In this they inherited a centuries-old Christian tradition, depicted prominently upon the great West-door of most cathedrals in Europe, and many in England. Queen *Ecclesia* (the Church) is shown as proud, triumphant and regal while *Synagoga* (Judaisms) is blind, defeated, sorrowful and ill clad. *Ecclesia* holds a banner but *Synagoga's* staff is broken.

**Plate 5a and 5b.** *Ecclasia* and *Synagoga* at Metz Cathedral.

Since the Middle Ages, large statues depicting this pair (each with her appropriate attributes) have been displayed in Bamberg, Strasbourg, Reims, Metz, Magdeburg, Freiburg, Minden, York, Lincoln, Rochester, Winchester, Salisbury, London and Norte Dame in Paris.

Calvin's associate, Ulrich Zwingli of Zurich (1484-1531) was a Protestant Reformer of a different stamp. He contested Catholics,

Luther and the radical's positions against the Jews. He had very little contact with any Jews as, in 1436, they had been expelled forever from Zurich for the honour of God and Mary, although he did know a Jewish doctor name Mosse. Zwingli believed that the widespread dispersion of the Jews was a divine punishment for Christ's crucifixion. Zwingli aimed to stay true to Scripture and he distinguished between the Jews of the Old Testament (the children of Israel) whom he regarded as true, biblical Jews and post-biblical, rabbinic Jews and contemporary Jews, who were "unbelievers". But he did not adopt the anti-Jewish polemic that was typical of his time, which he observed in Luther's invective.

There was also a movement in the 16th century, known as Christian Hebraism which Luther thought was dangerous and threatening. It was exemplified by the Hebrew scholar and grammarian, Sebastian Münster (1489-1552) and by Calvin's colleague, Martin Bucer (1491-1551) who looked to Jews for Old Testament exegesis. Luther read Christ into every possible Old Testament passage but they were concerned with the historical context of each of its various component books.

**Inquisitions: A Tool of the Catholic Counter-Reformation**

More detrimental in inciting deliberate anti-Semitic actions in Europe were the various Inquisituons, the most notorious and infamous of which was Spanish Inquisition, established under King Ferdinand and Queen Isabella of Spain in 1479. This was a major tool against those Jews and Moslems who refused to accept Roman Catholic baptism, or who continued in their former traditions. In the Iberian Peninsular this arm of the Catholic Church also punished, tortured and burnt Protestant 'heretics'.

**7) The King James Bible**

With the English Reformation came the need for every Christian to read the Bible, an activity which papal authority had discouraged or forbidden. A translation into English, the common tongue, was needed, which King James I, king of both Scotland and England, ordered to be undertaken in 1604. The Authorised Version was published in 1611 and to this day has remained the most widely read translation - greatly loved wherever English is spoken or studied.

Since the beginning, chapter and page headings, which describe or summarise the content of each section, have been included; in some editions in full, but in abbreviated form in other editions of the Bible. To many readers these headings have the authority of scripture, as though they were part of the text itself, and not simply a man-made convenience. The anti-Jewish bias of these notes has been a powerful, if somewhat unconscious force, in maintaining Christian anti-semitism and in preventing an objective understanding of the Biblical doctrine of Israel and the Church.

A quick glance at examples of page headings in, say, the Book of Isaiah, will give an indication of the extent of this negative influence:

Isaiah 30:"Gods's Mercies to his church."

Isaiah 34:"God revengeth his church"

Isaiah 35:"Blessings of the Gospel"

Isaiah 39:"Promulgation of the Gospel."

Isaiah 41:"His mercies to his church"

Isaiah 42:"The Office of Christ"

Isaiah 43:"God comforteth his church"

These headings are absurd because the Book of Isaiah is from the Tenach, the Hebrew Scriptures, and was written hundreds of years before the Church existed!!

But this is not all, let us look at some examples of where it is admitted, in these chapter headings, that Isaiah was actually speaking to Jews, or about Jews:

Isaiah 28: "Judgement upon Jerusalem"

Isaiah 29: "The Jews are reproved"

Isaiah 51: "Afflictions of Jerusalem"

Isaiah 59: "The sins of the Jews"

How amazing that Isaiah addresses a different readership in virtually every chapter!! How amazing that every negative heading, every reproof, was for the Jews, while the publishers attempted to indicate that Isaiah accorded to the Church every comfort, blessing, and mercy! Even when this translation of the Bible deals with the Epistle to the Romans, this same attitude is obvious. The paragraph headings for that great exposition of the Olive Tree metaphor, Chapter 9, includes these:

*"Paul's sorrow for the Jews"* ...."*The calling of the gentiles and rejection of the Jews"* and *"Why so few Jews embraced the righteousness of faith."*

With such attitudes appearing, written within the covers of the Bible, seeming, perhaps, to be coming from Paul's pen, is it any wonder that, throughout the centuries, readers have been confused, and have been unable to come to an appreciation of Paul's true argument?

## 8) The Spirit of Anti-Semitism

Members of the Church have been as much the victims of spiritual blindness as ever the Jews were. The humanistic spirit of anti-Christ, the work of the deceiver, the father of lies, robs Christians of a knowledge of the truth at every opportunity.

A short history of anti-Semitism indicates that at various periods of history, both devout believers and nominal Christians have behaved like their pagan predecessors, by being in the forefront of physical persecution of Jews.

A brief overview of the history of their persecution includes: their bondage in Egypt; in Assyria; in Babylon and by the Romans. It includes some of the Church Fathers Popes and Bishops previously mentioned; the Crusaders; the Spanish Inquisition; the Russian Pogroms; the Nazi Holocaust; the Stalinist purges and the Refuseniks' struggle of more recent years and their torments in, and expulsions from, Muslim majority lands. Thousands were slaughtered by rampaging Crusader knights, six million died under Adolf Hitler, and millions more under

Joseph Stalin. These are some of the excesses to which people have been driven by the evil spirit of anti-Semitism.

Nor is anti-semitism a thing of the distant past. Former Prime Minister Shamir's father died in a pogrom, violence against Jews continues in Moslem lands and in former communist countries and in the West violence not seen in living memory is occuring almost daily. Is it any wonder that it has penetrated modern Western societies, whipped up by pro-Palestinian rhetoric, and so the modern Church ?

With all these forces ranged against the Tenach, a few chapters from St.Paul's letters and a few verses from other Scriptures, is it surprising that the truth has almost been lost? But let us remind ourselves that God Almighty has said:

*"So shall my Word be that goeth forth out of my mouth: it shall not return unto me void, but it shall accomplish that which I please, and it shall prosper in the thing whereto I sent it."* (Is.55:11 A.V.)

May He send it to correct the errors of the centuries.

Plate 6. Camels carrying pruned olive branches
in 1900.
Photo: E and E. Marson. Public domain.

# Chapter 6
# Call and Gifts

In Romans Chapter 11, Paul looks forward to a day of salvation for the Jews, explaining that God's purpose and intention has always remained the same, unchanged. God's character is such that He does not change His mind when once He has chosen and promised. If God should fail to keep His covenants with Israel, and deny all of His good promises to them, there can be no assurance of salvation, no assurance of eternal love, in short, no assurance for the Church.

In the Old Testament the Jewish people were promised that they would not be forsaken, nor ultimately rejected; that indeed they are God's inheritance. They were also promised that their day of blessing would begin after they had been regathered into their ancient homeland:

> *"Therefore this is what the Sovereign Lord says: I will now bring Jacob back from captivity and will have compassion on all the people of Israel, and I will be zealous for my holy name ....*
>
> *When I have brought them back from the nations and have gathered them from the countries of their enemies, I will show myself holy through them in the sight of many nations.*
>
> *Then they will know that I am the Lord their God; for though I sent them into exile, among the nations, I will gather them to their own land, not leaving any behind.*
>
> *I will no longer hide my face from them, for I will pour out my Spirit on the House of Israel declares the Sovereign Lord."*
> (Ez.39:25, 27-29)

Paul confirms that God's gifts to Israel and the Divine call placed upon this people cannot be revoked. This obviously leads us to the question "*what constitutes these gifts and this call ?*"

**The Call**

The initial call of God came when Abram and Sarai were told to leave their home in Ur, near Babylon, and to journey to an unknown land of promise. They were also called to be the parents of a great nation, to establish a race of people who would worship the Lord Almighty; and they were called to bring blessing to all the peoples and families of the earth.

*"Leave your country, your people and your father's household and go to the land I will show you. I will make you into a great nation and I will bless you; I will make your name great, and you will be a blessing. I will bless those who bless you, and whoever curses you I will curse; and all peoples on earth will be blessed through you."*

(Gen.12:1b-3)

**The Gifts**

The first gift was a son in their old age, a 'son of promise', through whose lineage Abraham and Sarah's descendants would be as numerous as the sands on the seashore.

The second gift was the promise and the identification of a land to possess forever, (though, as Moses later explained, not necessarily to inhabit). This promise of a land was repeated again and again, to Abraham, to Isaac and to Jacob, as well as to Moses as he was viewing the land which he would never enter, (Deut.32:49). At Luz, in the Land of Canaan, God had spoken personally to Jacob, who was the third generation of the Patriarchs.

> *"'I am going to make you fruitful and will increase your numbers. I will make you a community of peoples, and I will give this land as an everlasting possession to your descendants after you.'" (Gen.48:4)*

The gift of ownership of the land was to endure for all time. The Land of Israel was their permanent inheritance. So seriously did God view this gift that He gave it by covenant (Gen.15:18); and Paul confirms that this covenant cannot be broken, nor ever annulled. Its survival does not depend upon the Law of Moses as it was made hundreds of years before the Law was given, in fact, while Abraham was still uncircumcised, still, as it were, a 'gentile'.

> *"What I mean is this: The law, introduced 430 years later, does not set aside the covenant previously established by God and thus do away with the promise. For if the inheritance depends on the law, then it no longer depends on a promise; but God in his grace gave it to Abraham through a promise."*

(Gal.3:17-18)

Paul, in Galatians Chapter 3, reinforces the idea that this covenant is perpetual, by saying that, just as human covenants cannot be set aside, how much more so a covenant made by God.

Although ownership of the land was perpetual, occupancy of it depended upon faithfulness and obedience. Banishment from the land was a consequence to which God may resort and in fact did resort, in order to punish and to call the people's hearts back to Himself. Expulsion from the land was never meant to be permanent, and certainly it was not in any way an annulment of the gift of the land! Not only this, but a further gift, a spiritual gift, was promised. This gift would enable the people to have such a right attitude to the Lord that they would never again have to be punished by banishment from the Land.

This is the ultimate gift, the New Covenant, which was initially promised, not first through Jeremiah, but during the first Exodus.

> *"The Lord your God will circumcise your hearts and the hearts of your descendants, so that you may love him with all your heart and with all your soul, and live... You again will obey the Lord and follow all the commands I am giving you today.*
>
> *The Lord will again delight in you and make you prosperous, just as he delighted in your fathers."* (Deut.30:6,8,9b)

So significant is the promise of this gift that, not only Moses, but Jeremiah, Isaiah, Ezekiel and Zechariah spoke at length about the wonder and blessing that it would ultimately bring to the people of Israel. Here is the best known example:

> *"` This the covenant that I will make with the House of Israel after that time.' declares the Lord 'I will put my law in their minds and write it on their hearts. I will be their God and they will be my people'".* (Jer.31:33)

A most wonderful gift was the Lord's promise to be a father and a shepherd to them, as well as their holy and mighty God. The gods of all the nations around were seen as aloof, detached, but the God of Israel self-described as a God who will shepherd His people on the rich pastures of the mountains of Israel, in their own Land:

> *"They will know that I, the Lord their God, am with them and that they, the house of Israel, are my people, declares the Sovereign Lord. You my sheep, the sheep of my pasture, are my people, and I am your God, declares the Sovereign Lord."* (Ez.34:30-31).

# Chapter 7
# The Second Metaphor

Imagery based on trees is also used by Paul in the second metaphor of this epistle, the `Branch metaphor', which similarly borrows its imagery and theology from the *Tenach*, and especially from the prophet Isaiah. This second metaphor is similar to the Olive Tree metaphor in that it also demonstrates that the promises of the Old Testament are reaffirmed as belonging to the Jewish people, the people of the Covenant of Circumcision.

Although there are similarities between the doctrines which these two metaphors serve to illustrate, in that they both refer to Jews and Gentiles, the two metaphors must not be confused by the reader. The second metaphor is found in Romans Chapter 15 and it refers to a teaching about Jesus, the Messiah or Christ.

Jesus is identified by Paul as that mysterious Messianic figure whom the prophets called `The Branch'. Paul, in expounding the second `tree' metaphor, wrote that the Messiah will "shoot up from the stump of Jesse" - (Jesse, of course, was David's father). `The Branch' would therefore be of David's lineage. In this metaphor we have the picture of a felled or heavily pruned fruit tree. Only the root and stump remain; yet the life within that tree causes a side shoot to grow up, to flourish and to bear fruit. An example of this comes from the Garden of Gethsemane whose ancient olive trees are believed to have grown from the stumps of the very same trees under which Jesus prayed, but which the Roman army cut down. Olive trees do not die with age, new suckers simply grow up beside the old trunk, renewing the life of the tree, so that a shoot can grow up and bear fruit. David had been promised a perpetual throne, rulers from Jesse's line; but it did appear that the royal line was cut off; as dead and unfruitful as a tree stump. But those, like Paul, who knew the Hebrew scriptures, knew that it was foretold that new life would come forth, a king would emerge, upon whom the Spirit of the Lord would rest in wisdom, justice and righteousness. Yeshua, Jesus, was of David's line. Scholars generally believe, in fact, that Yeshua was descended from David through both Mary's and Joseph's lines, as if to underline his royal descent:

> *"In that day the Root of Jesse will stand as a banner for the peoples; the nations will rally to him, and his place of rest will be glorious. In that day the Lord will reach out his hand a second time to reclaim the remnant that is left of his people from Assyria, from Lower Egypt, from Upper Egypt, from Cush, from Elam, from Babylonia, from Hamath and from the islands of the sea. He will raise a banner for the nations and will gather the exiles of Israel; he will assemble the scattered people of Judah from the four quarters of the earth."* (Is.11:10-12)

In Romans 15:8, Paul writes that God in His mercy has, in the Christian era, not abolished, but confirmed His promises made to the Patriarchs of old:

> *"For I tell you that Christ (Messiah) has become a servant of the Jews on behalf of God's truth to confirm the promises made to the patriarchs so that the Gentiles may glorify God for his mercy."* (Rom.15:8-9)

Paul also declares here that the Gentiles SHARE in the Jews' spiritual blessings; not that they take those blessings away from the Jews, (Rom.15:27). In this chapter there is also a profound but rarely acknowledged teaching, that the material prosperity of the Gentiles should, indeed must, be shared with the Jews; and this is NOT limited only to the Jewish believers:

*"For if the Gentiles have shared in the Jews' spiritual blessings, they owe it to the Jews to share with them their material blessings."* (Rom.15:27)

This truly Biblical teaching is rarely acted upon, and even more rarely taught from church pulpits.

**Plate 7. Garden of Gethsemane c.1900,
Charles Warren, 'Picturesque Palestine Sinai and Egyt'**

# Chapter 8
# In That Day

'That day' and 'those days' are Biblical expressions which mean the 'last days' or the 'end-of-days'. The original Call of Abraham, the founding father of Israel, has already been discussed, but there remain many other elements of 'The Call'.

The people of Israel have not, as yet, responded fully to these, and some aspects of the Call upon Israel will only be fulfilled by Israel in the end-of-days.

These include:

(1) The call to holiness and priestly service;

(2) the call to world-wide service; and

(3) the call to marriage.

## (1) Priestly Service

Since the destruction of the Second Temple in 70 A.D the full meaning of priestly ministry has been lost both by Jews, who see their rabbis only as teachers, as well as by Christians, who understand their clergy to be those who minister to the people. Rather than being primarily concerned with the various needs of the congregation, the priests of the Lord ministered UNTO THE LORD. This was their primary responsibility, their highest calling.

On behalf of the people, once a year, one of their number, the High Priest, duly purified himself and then ministered within the dark inner enclosure called the Holy of Holies. The ministry of atonement is the most awesome and responsible that any mortal man has ever been selected to perform.

As Leviticus Chapter 10 shows, incorrect observance could have meant instant death. On Yom Kippur, the Day of Atonement, the High Priest was the most totally alone of men. His solemn and solitary duty was to purchase forgiveness of sin for all Israel, through the sprinkling of the blood of one of the pure sacrificial goats upon the Mercy Seat, where the Shekinah Glory dwelt. This sacrifice, if correctly offered, obtained temporary, annual forgiveness of Israel's sin, while the guilt of conscience was placed upon the Scapegoat and carried far away, into the wilderness. The High Priest's function contained many elements. He was the intermediary between God and man. He ministered to the Almighty before the Shekinah - His Holy Presence. He offered prayer, represented by the incense which he offered behind the veil on this one day of the year, on behalf of the people.

The Jewish rabbis now teach that personal suffering, good works, the merits of the righteous, and of the Patriarchs, and even one's own death, with repentance, are redemptive. But some feel such a need for a blood atonement that, in their homes on Yom Kippur, they perform `Kapparot', the slaughter of a white cock or hen for each person, saying: *"this is my substitute; this is in exchange for me; this is my atonement."* This ritual, performed totally outside of the regulations of Biblical Law, the Torah, fulfils the words of the prophet Hosea:

> *"For the Israelites will live many days without king or prince, without sacrifice .... without ephod."* (Hos.3:4)

Death remains the punishment of sin (Rom.6:23), but even in the absence of the scapegoat as a sacrifice of atonement, Yom Kippur ceases to be a day of tragedy because God's gift is life through the blood of Messiah:

> *"But he was pierced for our transgressions, he was crushed for our iniquities.... and the Lord has laid on him the iniquity of us all."*
> (Is.53:5a,6b)

The priests of the Lord were not selected just from the tribe of Levi but had to be descended from Aaron, Moses' brother, through-out the genealogies of both of their parents. Yet even in the Tenach there was the knowledge that the whole House of Israel was intended to be a holy people, to fulfil a priestly function, and also that someday they would do so.

*"And they (the survivors) will bring all your brothers, from all the nations, to my holy mountain in Jerusalem as an offering to the Lord....... They will bring them, as the Israelites bring their grain offerings, to the temple of the Lord in ceremonially clean vessels. And I will select some of them also to be priests and Levites,' says the Lord."* (Is.66:20-21).

When this comes to pass Jerusalem will be called the "*City no longer deserted*" and the people of Israel will be holy, called by the name, "*redeemed of the Lord*", (Is.62:12).

*"They will be called oaks of righteousness, a planting of the Lord for the display of his splendour.... And you will be called priests of the Lord, you will be named ministers of our God".* (Is.61:3b & 6a)

In the highest heavens the high priestly function is being fulfilled perpetually, by Jesus our eternal High Priest.

*"He did not enter by means of the blood of goats and calves; but he entered the Most Holy Place once for all by his own blood, having obtained eternal redemption."* (Heb.9:12)

In view of the work of Yeshua, our Great High Priest, why is an earthly priestly service still part of the Divine Intention?

Although the atonement has been offered, the other priestly functions continue. These include the offering of prayers and praise and the ministry to the Lord. Like the gifts of God, the call of Israel to holiness and priestly service has not been revoked.

### (2) The Call to Serve The Nations.

From the very beginning of the nation of Israel as an identifiable and distinct people, they were called to serve the Lord and to fulfil a unique and God-given function for the benefit of their fellow men, the Gentiles. At the time of the original call of Abraham, God explained that this was a call to obedient service. The testing of Abraham, on Mt. Moriah, recounted in Genesis 22:2, was a test of his obedience, a test of Abraham's servanthood. He, and his son Isaac gave unquestioning obedience. Thus they demonstrated true servanthood; for a servant does not resist his master's orders, nor ask 'why'.

Like Mary, the mother of Jesus, Abraham was visited by the Angel of the Lord who made a momentous announcement, a powerful Divine affirmation. Abraham, like Mary, answered the Angelic Messenger with a response of submissive servanthood. At two moments of crisis Abraham simply and calmly responded to the Lord:

*"Here I am."* (Gen.22:1b & 11b)

The Lord Almighty responded to Abraham's obedience with blessings; blessings for his offspring, and blessings for the nations:

> " `I sware by myself,' declares the Lord, 'that because you have done this and have not withheld your son, your only son, I will surely bless you .... and through your off-spring all nations on earth will be blest, because you obeyed me'."* (Gen.22:16-18)

Gradually, throughout the Tenach, God revealed the details of the call to servant-hood placed upon Abraham's descendants. The prophet Isaiah developed the idea of Israel as a people called to belong to the Lord. This included the call to be:

   i.   The Lord's Servant. (Is.44:21)
   ii.   A Light to the Gentiles. (Is.49:6)
   iii.   A Covenant for the people. (Is.42:6)
   iv.   to Show the Lord's glory.(Is.44:23) and
   v.   to Proclaim His Praise. (Is.43:21)

Judaism is not seen as a deliberately proselytizing religion, yet by its very nature it has always attracted proselytes, and continues to attract them. In New Testament times these people played a key role. They were often called `God-fearers' and were noted for their zeal, generosity and purity of life. Throughout history there have been relatively few of them, but the prophet Isaiah announced that in the last days many from Israel will be sent out to the most remote islands, to heathen nations, for a God ordained purpose, the proclamation of His Glory and of His message to the Gentiles.

*"I will set a sign among them, and I will send some of those who survive to the nations - to Tarshish, to the Libyans and Lydians.... and to the distant islands that have not heard of my fame or seen my glory. They will proclaim my glory among the nations."* (Is.66:19)

In the New Testament, in the Revelation, John provides a glimpse of the success of their endeavors in reaching all the nations of earth with this message. After detailing the list of representatives of each of the twelve tribes of Israel, 144,000 in all, who had come out of the tribulation and whose foreheads were sealed with the seal of the Living God, John wrote:

*"... I looked and there before me was a great multitude that no-one could count, from every nation, tribe, people, and language standing before the throne and in front of the Lamb".* (Rev.7:9a)

It will be as Isaiah has said: after the tribes of Israel have been restored to the Lord they will serve Him, even at the ends of the earth:

*"He says: 'It is too small a thing for you to be my servant to restore the tribes of Jacob and bring back those of Israel I have kept. I will also make you a light for the Gentiles, that you may bring my salvation to the ends of the earth.'"* (Is.49:6)

In that day the people of Israel will indeed fulfil both the call to a worldwide spiritual service among the Gentiles and the call to the priestly service of praise and of the declaration of the Glory of the Lord.

## (3) The Marriage Call

The life of the prophet Hosea was a parable in action; a prophetic message lived out over a period of many years. Each detail of Hosea's family life was in direct obedience to the Lord's commands. Each was accompanied by a prophetic message which explained the parable. The people of Israel were left in no doubt as to why Hosea behaved in ways which were sometimes contrary to those expected of a prophet of God; for example in selecting a harlot for a wife. By this means Israel was clearly told and demonstrably shown that they too were unfaithful, an unfaithful wife to the Lord.

Hosea's prophetic message was not simply metaphorical; that Israel was LIKE an unfaithful wife; but that Israel IS a wife. Nor is Hosea alone in conveying this astonishing concept - that Israel is a wife to the Lord. The prophet Isaiah concurs:

*"For your Maker is your husband - the Lord Almighty is his name - the Holy One of Israel is your Redeemer; he is called the God of all the Earth."* (Is.54:5)

Even though it did appear that Israel had been cast off; forever rejected because of her spiritual adultery; the Lord's compassion prevented Him from this step:

*"How can I give you up, Ephraim? How can I hand you over, Israel? ...my heart is changed within me; all my compassion is aroused...."* (Hos.11:8)

Although Israel, the wife, had given herself over to another, given into servitude, she will be purchased back by her husband, whatever the cost.

*"'Fear not, for I have redeemed you; I have called you by name; you are mine..... Since you are precious and honored in my sight, and because I love you, I will give men in exchange for you, and people in exchange for your life.'"* (Is.43:1a & 4)

Just as Hosea ransomed his wife, Gomer, from bondage, and restored her to his family and his home, so Israel, although unfaithful - having broken her relationship with her Heavenly Husband - will be redeemed, courted again, and allured by Him. Then she will no longer be in bondage or servitude, she will be restored to the status of 'wife'.

We are so used to the New Testament concept of "the Bride, the Lamb's Wife", from Rev.19:9, that it is difficult to think about another Scriptural husband-wife relationship. It is equally difficult to accept that such is based upon a God-given covenant: but this is what the Tenach teaches. God's love is demonstrated in this marriage covenant, which is similar to the Jewish marriage contract, defining the roles, the relationship and the commitment. Like the marriage of the Lamb it is an eternal covenant made by the Holy One, the Keeper of Covenants.

*"Know therefore that the Lord your God is God; he is the faithful God, keeping his covenant of love to a thousand generations of those who love him and keep his commands."* (Deut.7:9)

Pause for a moment to consider what it means when the Lord Almighty promises to enter into a covenant. It means that His honour,

His faithfulness, His very nature is bound up with that promise. His honour and His truth are bound up with His marriage covenant promises. Our faith in the coming marriage of the Bride, the Lamb's Wife, depends upon God's faithfulness to the wife of His marriage covenant.

How does the Lord describe this marriage covenant?

> *"In that day I will make a covenant for them ...... I will betroth you to me forever; I will betroth you in righteousness and justice, in love and compassion. I will betroth you in faithfulness, and you will acknowledge the Lord." (Hos.2:18a,19-20)*

The Call to Marriage is a beautiful one, requiring a response of fidelity and devotion. The people who once seemed unloved will be drawn back into a love relationship by the Holy One. His wife, Israel, will be once again bound to Him in a love-covenant which He has written, and to which they will respond with devotion and gratitude.

This call to marital restoration awaits its appointed time, its time of fulfilment. The Tenach identifies this time as the 'end-of-days'. That day is not passed, it is not a finished dispensation but a future era. The God of Israel intends that His wife, His treasured possession, should flourish like an enduring and fruitful olive tree, bringing the oil of joy and anointing to many. Of Israel He announces:

> *"His splendour will be like an olive tree, his fragrance like a cedar of Lebanon." (Hos.14:6)*

And this is not all, the Heavenly Husband adds:

> *"I will heal their waywardness and love them freely." (Hos. 14:4a)*

Plate 8. Women crush whole olives,
the first of a two step progess.
The second is to squeeze oil out of the pulp.

# Chapter 9
# The Mystery Solved

A divine mystery concerning His two Olive Trees was created in the secret council of the Holy One of Israel long before Abraham was chosen. It is the mystery of Divine selection and the granting of Divine mercy. The Apostle Paul explained this mystery because ignorance of its meaning was not desirable, nor part of the Lord's intention.

**Plate 9. One of Jerusalem's oldest olive trees.
Photo: Ian Finnin, 2018.**

God's Ancient Covenant People, the first chosen people, had to be kept apart from the contaminating influence of the various pagan religions of the Middle East, whose practices included and extremes of sexual debauchery, and human and infant sacrifice. This meant, in effect, that Israel kept aloof, exclusive, separated from the Gentiles to whom they were meant to be a light, an example, a teacher. It couldn't be any other way. Every time Israel came into close contact with pagans they departed from the Lord, adopting heathen practices which were detestable to

Him, and falling into gross wickedness. This endangered their racial and religious survival. Their existence as a race would have succumbed because of intermarriage, venereal disease, homosexuality, human sacrifice, murder, and infanticide. Their religious survival was threatened by hardness of heart, following false prophets, syncretism with other beliefs, idol worship, the departure of the Lord's anointing, and God's judgements, such as their dispersion among the nations.

Messiah, the Root of Jesse's line, was threatened by evil long before Herod's merciless slaughter of the tiny boys of Bethlehem. The Holy Seed was threatened when Hebrew midwives were ordered to kill newborn boys, when babies were thrown into the River Nile, when Hebrew captives were taken away as slaves, and when Haman attempted to annihilate their race. It was threatened every time a golden calf, an altar of Baal or an Ashtoreth pole tempted the people away from the Living God. Ultimate redemption for all mankind was threatened throughout the history of Ancient Israel whenever any Hebrew heart turned away from the worship of Yahweh, when any man from the tribe of Judah, especially from David's royal line, was seduced into a pagan marriage by an attractive 'Delilah'. Their separation was vital for their survival, but that excluded most of the remainder of mankind, who were thus alienated from a knowledge of the God of Mercy and Justice.

This exclusiveness meant, in effect, that the knowledge of the One True God would have been reserved as exclusively Israel's prerogative, had it not been for the *"hardening in part"* (Rom.11:25), which soon compelled the disciples to take the Truth to more receptive audiences; out of the synagogues and into the streets. So mercy will be shown to the Gentiles, continually, until their full number has been gathered in. Although previously excluded, they are now welcome to join the Commonwealth of Israel. The Lord admonished Gentile believers in Jesus, the Jewish Messiah to remember:

*"That .... ye were without Christ (Messiah) being aliens from the commonwealth of Israel, and strangers from the covenants of promise , having no hope and without God in the world ....... Now therefore ye are no more strangers and foreigners, but fellow citizens with the saints, and of the household of God."* (Eph.2:12 and 19, K.J.V.)

God chose to show mercy to the Gentiles, the Wild Olive Tree, accepting them equally. Israel was the Lord's first family, yet He chose, in the fullness of time, according to His purposes, to adopt Gentiles into His family. He added His adopted children, His sons and daughters from among the Gentiles, to the family while keeping His promises to His original children.

*"If you belong to Christ, then you are Abraham's seed, and heirs according to the promise."*

(Gal. 3:29).

Each of these two people-groups has its own unique nature and role, yet they are equally loved, equal recipients of the Father's blessing and equal inheritors of the family fortunes.

*"... ye have received the Spirit of adoption, whereby we cry, Abba, Father. The Spirit itself beareth witness with our spirit, that we are the children of God. And if children, then heirs; heirs of God, and joint-heirs with Christ (Messiah)."*

(Rom.8:15b-17a, K.J.V.)

The olive tree
Is no longer a mystery,

Nor solely a metaphor,
It is a family.

# USEFUL BIBLIOGRAPHY


Bagatti, Bellarmino OFM (Eugene Hoade OFM, trans.), *The Church from the Circumcision History and Archaeology of the Judaeo-Christians* (Jerusalem: Franciscan Printing Press, 1971/1984/2004).

Bauckham, Richard, *Jude and the Relatives of Jesus in the Early Church* (Edinburgh: T and T Clark, 1990).
——-*Jesus and the Eye-witnesses:*
*The Gospels as Eyewitness Testimony* 2$^{nd}$ ed.
(Grand Rapids, MI: Eerdmans, 2006/2014).

Dunn, J. D. G. (ed.), *Jews and Christians: the Parting of the Ways* A.D.70-135 The Second Durham-Tubingen Research Symposium on Earliest Christianity and Judaism, Durham, Sept., 1989. (Tubingen: Mohr, 1992).

Jansen, Hans, 'The Historical Roots of the Anti-Israel Position of Liberal Protestant Churches,'
*Jerusalem Centre for Security and Foreign Affairs*
(*JCFA*) 57.1 (2007).
Linder, Amnon, *The Jews in Roman Imperial Legislation*).
(Detroit, MI and Israel Academy of Science and Humanities, Jerusalem: Wayne State University Press, 1987).
Olsson, Berger and Magnus Zetterholm (eds), *The Ancient Synagogue From its Origins until 200 C.E*
(Stockholm, 2003).
Perry, Marvin and Frederick M. Schweitzer (eds), *Jewish-Christian Encounters over the Centuries: Symbiosis, Prejudice, Holocaust, Dialogue.*

(New York, Peter Lang, 1994).
Rokeah, David, *Justin Martyr and the Jews*
(Leiden: Brill, 2002).
Rosenthal, Frank, 'The Rise of Christian Hebraism
in the Sixteenth Century',
*Historia Judaica* 7 (1945), 167-191.


Schlauch, Margartet, 'The Allegory of Church and Synagogue',
*Speculum* 14.4 (1975), 448-464.
Simon, Marcel, (H. McKeating, trans.), *Verus Israel*
(London: Vallentine Mitchell, 1907/1986/1996).
Thompson, Mark, 'Luther and the Jews',
*Reformed Theological Review* 67 (2008), 121-145.
*Winter, Ralph D. and Steven Hawthorne (eds), Perspectives on the
World Christian Movement: A Reader, 3rd edition (Pasadena: William
Carey Library, 1981/1999).*
Wilken, Robert L., *John Chrysostom and the Jews: Rhetoric in the
Late Fourth Century* (Berkeley: University of California Press, 1983).
Williamson, Clark W., *Has God Rejected His People? Anti-Judaism in
the Christian Church* (Nashville: Abingdon, 1982).


**Electronic sources**


Kirn, Hans-Martin, 'Ulrich Zwingli, the Jews and Judaism'
https://brill.com/display/book/89047408851/89047408851_s//
Olsen, Daphne M, 'Luther and Hitler: A Linear Connection
between Martin Luther and Adolf Hitler's Anti-Semitism with a
Nationalistic Foundation' *(2012) Master of Libedral Studies Thesis, 20
Htttps://scholarship.rollins.edu/mls/20*

Pak, G. Sujin. 'The Protestant Reformers and the Jews: Excavating Contexts, Unearthing Logic.'
https://doi.org/10.3390/rel8040072

# Don't miss out!

Visit the website below and you can sign up to receive emails whenever Deslee Campbell publishes a new book. There's no charge and no obligation.

https://books2read.com/r/B-A-LSULB-BJUAF

BOOKS2READ

Connecting independent readers to independent writers.

# Also by Deslee Campbell

**Memorable Christians**
Phoebe's Sister's: Women Leaders in Early Christianity
Phoebe's Sisters: Women Leaders in Early Christianity
Phoebe's Sisters : Women Leaders in Early Christianity
Bright Shining Lights of an Earlier Era
Shining Lights of the Reformation
Shining Lights of the Reformation
Remarkable Post-Reformation Christians
Remarkable Post-Reformation Christians
Remarkable Post-Reformation Christians
Modern Christian Martyrs
Modern Christian Martyrs
Modern Christian Martyrs
Modern Christian Martyrs ready.doc
Christian Women We Should Remember
Great Christian Men We Have Forgotten
Great Christian Men We Have Forgotten
Great Christian Men We Have Forgotten
Christian Women Leaders of the 20th Century

**Shoah Series**
Confronting Holocaust Denial

**Standalone**
The Topkapi Beggar
Voices From The Silence
Why a Roman Emperor Rebuilt Jerusalem and Jerash
Why a Roman Emperor Rebuilt Jerusalem and Jerash
Stones, Walls and Watchmen
Mothers in Israel
Ecclesia a Long Journey to Tomorrow
St Paul's Olive Tree Metaphor
St Paul's Olive Tree Metaphor

Watch for more at www.synagogueandchurch.com.

# About the Author

About the Author

Dr Deslee Campbell, a retired educational psychologist and teacher, is a prolific writer of both fiction and works concerned with history, religion and archaeology. She is particularly interested in art, artefacts and architecture as pathways towards understanding the past. Her doctoral thesis from the University of Sydney is entitled "The Iconography of Women: A Study of Byzantium and the Byzantine-influenced Mediterranean, A.D. 395-1204."

Read more at https://www.youtube.com/@synagogueandchurch911.

www.ingramcontent.com/pod-product-compliance
Lightning Source LLC
Chambersburg PA
CBHW051255160726
47994CB00003B/1172